'HIS TONGUE IS THE PRICK OF A DEVIL.'

ALLEN GINSBERG
Born 1926, New Jersey, USA
Died 1997, New York, USA

All these poems are taken from *Collected Poems 1947–1997*,
first published in 2006.

GINSBERG IN PENGUIN MODERN CLASSICS
Collected Poems 1947–1997
The Essential Ginsberg
Howl, Kaddish and Other Poems
Selected Poems 1947–1995
Wait Till I'm Dead

ALLEN GINSBERG

Television Was a Baby Crawling Toward That Deathchamber

PENGUIN BOOKS

PENGUIN CLASSICS

UK | USA | Canada | Ireland | Australia
India | New Zealand | South Africa

Penguin Books is part of the Penguin Random House group
of companies whose addresses can be found at
global.penguinrandomhouse.com.

This selection first published 2018

007

Copyright © Allen Ginsberg, 1996

Set in 10.25/12.75 pt Dante MT Std
Typeset by Jouve (UK), Milton Keynes

Printed and bound in Great Britain by Clays Ltd, Elcograf S.p.A.

ISBN: 978–0–241–33762–2

www.greenpenguin.co.uk

Contents

Pull My Daisy

Pull my daisy
tip my cup
all my doors are open
Cut my thoughts
for coconuts
all my eggs are broken
Jack my Arden
gate my shades
woe my road is spoken
Silk my garden
rose my days
now my prayers awaken

Bone my shadow
dove my dream
start my halo bleeding
Milk my mind &
make me cream
drink me when you're ready
Hop my heart on
harp my height
seraphs hold me steady
Hip my angel

hype my light
lay it on the needy

Heal the raindrop
sow the eye
bust my dust again
Woe the worm
work the wise
dig my spade the same
Stop the hoax
what's the hex
where's the wake
how's the hicks
take my golden beam

Rob my locker
lick my rocks
leap my cock in school
Rack my lacks
lark my looks
jump right up my hole
Whore my door
beat my boor
eat my snake of fool
Craze my hair
bare my poor
asshole shorn of wool

Say my oops
ope my shell
bite my naked nut
Roll my bones
ring my bell
call my worm to sup
Pope my parts
pop my pot
raise my daisy up
Poke my pap
pit my plum
let my gap be shut

Allen Ginsberg, Jack Kerouac & Neal Cassady
New York, Spring–Fall 1949

A Supermarket in California

What thoughts I have of you tonight, Walt Whitman, for I walked down the sidestreets under the trees with a headache self-conscious looking at the full moon.

In my hungry fatigue, and shopping for images, I went into the neon fruit supermarket, dreaming of your enumerations!

What peaches and what penumbras! Whole families shopping at night! Aisles full of husbands! Wives in the avocados, babies in the tomatoes! – and you, García Lorca, what were you doing down by the watermelons?

I saw you, Walt Whitman, childless, lonely old grubber, poking among the meats in the refrigerator and eyeing the grocery boys.

I heard you asking questions of each: Who killed the pork chops? What price bananas? Are you my Angel?

I wandered in and out of the brilliant stacks of cans following you, and followed in my imagination by the store detective.

We strode down the open corridors together in our solitary fancy tasting artichokes, possessing every frozen delicacy, and never passing the cashier.

Where are we going, Walt Whitman? The doors close in an hour. Which way does your beard point tonight?

(I touch your book and dream of our odyssey in the supermarket and feel absurd.)

Will we walk all night through solitary streets? The trees add shade to shade, lights out in the houses, we'll both be lonely.

Will we stroll dreaming of the lost America of love past blue automobiles in driveways, home to our silent cottage?

Ah, dear father, graybeard, lonely old courage-teacher, what America did you have when Charon quit poling his ferry and you got out on a smoking bank and stood watching the boat disappear on the black waters of Lethe?

Berkeley, 1955

America

America I've given you all and now I'm nothing.
America two dollars and twentyseven cents January 17, 1956.
I can't stand my own mind.
America when will we end the human war?
Go fuck yourself with your atom bomb.
I don't feel good don't bother me.
I won't write my poem till I'm in my right mind.
America when will you be angelic?
When will you take off your clothes?
When will you look at yourself through the grave?
When will you be worthy of your million Trotskyites?
America why are your libraries full of tears?
America when will you send your eggs to India?
I'm sick of your insane demands.
When can I go into the supermarket and buy what I need with
    my good looks?
America after all it is you and I who are perfect not the next
    world.
Your machinery is too much for me.
You made me want to be a saint.
There must be some other way to settle this argument.
Burroughs is in Tangiers I don't think he'll come back it's sinister.
Are you being sinister or is this some form of practical joke?
I'm trying to come to the point.

I refuse to give up my obsession.

America stop pushing I know what I'm doing.

America the plum blossoms are falling.

I haven't read the newspapers for months, everyday somebody
goes on trial for murder.

America I feel sentimental about the Wobblies.

America I used to be a communist when I was a kid I'm not sorry.

I smoke marijuana every chance I get.

I sit in my house for days on end and stare at the roses in the
closet.

When I go to Chinatown I get drunk and never get laid.

My mind is made up there's going to be trouble.

You should have seen me reading Marx.

My psychoanalyst thinks I'm perfectly right.

I won't say the Lord's Prayer.

I have mystical visions and cosmic vibrations.

America I still haven't told you what you did to Uncle Max
after he came over from Russia.

I'm addressing you.

Are you going to let your emotional life be run by Time
Magazine?

I'm obsessed by Time Magazine.

I read it every week.

Its cover stares at me every time I slink past the corner
candystore.

I read it in the basement of the Berkeley Public Library.

It's always telling me about responsibility. Businessmen are
serious. Movie producers are serious. Everybody's
serious but me.

It occurs to me that I am America.
I am talking to myself again.

Asia is rising against me.
I haven't got a chinaman's chance.
I'd better consider my national resources.
My national resources consist of two joints of marijuana
      millions of genitals an unpublishable private literature
      that jetplanes 1400 miles an hour and twentyfive-
      thousand mental institutions.
I say nothing about my prisons nor the millions of underprivil-
      eged who live in my flowerpots under the light of five
      hundred suns.
I have abolished the whorehouses of France, Tangiers is the
      next to go.
My ambition is to be President despite the fact that I'm a
      Catholic.

America how can I write a holy litany in your silly mood?
I will continue like Henry Ford my strophes are as individual
      as his automobiles more so they're all different sexes.
America I will sell you strophes $2500 apiece $500 down on
      your old strophe
America free Tom Mooney
America save the Spanish Loyalists
America Sacco & Vanzetti must not die
America I am the Scottsboro boys.
America when I was seven momma took me to Communist
      Cell meetings they sold us garbanzos a handful per ticket

a ticket costs a nickel and the speeches were free every-
    body was angelic and sentimental about the workers it
    was all so sincere you have no idea what a good thing the
    party was in 1835 Scott Nearing was a grand old man a real
    mensch Mother Bloor the Silk-strikers' Ewig-Weibliche
    made me cry I once saw the Yiddish orator Israel Amter
    plain. Everybody must have been a spy.
America you don't really want to go to war.
America it's them bad Russians.
Them Russians them Russians and them Chinamen. And them
    Russians.
The Russia wants to eat us alive. The Russia's power mad. She
    wants to take our cars from out our garages.
Her wants to grab Chicago. Her needs a Red *Reader's
    Digest*. Her wants our auto plants in Siberia. Him big
    bureaucracy running our fillingstations.
That no good. Ugh. Him make Indians learn read. Him need
    big black niggers. Hah. Her make us all work sixteen
    hours a day. Help.
America this is quite serious.
America this is the impression I get from looking in the
    television set.
America is this correct?
I'd better get right down to the job.
It's true I don't want to join the Army or turn lathes in precision
    parts factories, I'm nearsighted and psychopathic anyway.
America I'm putting my queer shoulder to the wheel.

Berkeley, January 17, 1956

Death to Van Gogh's Ear!

POET is Priest
Money has reckoned the soul of America
Congress broken thru to the precipice of Eternity
the President built a War machine which will vomit and rear
    up Russia out of Kansas
The American Century betrayed by a mad Senate which no
    longer sleeps with its wife
Franco has murdered Lorca the fairy son of Whitman
just as Mayakovsky committed suicide to avoid Russia
Hart Crane distinguished Platonist committed suicide to cave
    in the wrong America
just as millions of tons of human wheat were burned in secret
    caverns under the White House
while India starved and screamed and ate mad dogs full of rain
and mountains of eggs were reduced to white powder in the
    halls of Congress
no godfearing man will walk there again because of the stink of
    the rotten eggs of America
and the Indians of Chiapas continue to gnaw their vitaminless
    tortillas
aborigines of Australia perhaps gibber in the eggless wilderness
and I rarely have an egg for breakfast tho my work requires
    infinite eggs to come to birth in Eternity
eggs should be eaten or given to their mothers

and the grief of the countless chickens of America is expressed
     in the screaming of her comedians over the radio
Detroit has built a million automobiles of rubber trees and
     phantoms
but I walk, I walk, and the Orient walks with me, and all Africa
     walks
and sooner or later North America will walk
for as we have driven the Chinese Angel from our door he will
     drive us from the Golden Door of the future
we have not cherished pity on Tanganyika
Einstein alive was mocked for his heavenly politics
Bertrand Russell driven from New York for getting laid
immortal Chaplin driven from our shores with the rose in his
     teeth
a secret conspiracy by Catholic Church in the lavatories of
     Congress has denied contraceptives to the unceasing
     masses of India.
Nobody publishes a word that is not the cowardly robot
     ravings of a depraved mentality
The day of the publication of the true literature of the
     American body will be day of Revolution
the revolution of the sexy lamb
the only bloodless revolution that gives away corn
poor Genet will illuminate the harvesters of Ohio
Marijuana is a benevolent narcotic but J. Edgar Hoover prefers
     his deathly scotch
And the heroin of Lao-Tze & the Sixth Patriarch is punished
     by the electric chair
but the poor sick junkies have nowhere to lay their heads

fiends in our government have invented a cold-turkey cure
    for addiction as obsolete as the Defense Early Warning
    Radar System.
I am the defense early warning radar system
I see nothing but bombs
I am not interested in preventing Asia from being Asia
and the governments of Russia and Asia will rise and fall but
    Asia and Russia will not fall
the government of America also will fall but how can
    America fall
I doubt if anyone will ever fall anymore except governments
fortunately all the governments will fall
the only ones which won't fall are the good ones
and the good ones don't yet exist
But they have to begin existing they exist in my poems
they exist in the death of the Russian and American
    governments
they exist in the death of Hart Crane & Mayakovsky
Now is the time for prophecy without death as a consequence
the universe will ultimately disappear
Hollywood will rot on the windmills of Eternity
Hollywood whose movies stick in the throat of God
Yes Hollywood will get what it deserves
Time
Seepage of nerve-gas over the radio
History will make this poem prophetic and its awful silliness
    a hideous spiritual music
I have the moan of doves and the feather of ecstasy
Man cannot long endure the hunger of the cannibal abstract

War is abstract
the world will be destroyed
but I will die only for poetry, that will save the world
Monument to Sacco & Vanzetti not yet financed to ennoble
      Boston
natives of Kenya tormented by idiot con-men from England
South Africa in the grip of the white fool
Vachel Lindsay Secretary of the Interior
Poe Secretary of Imagination
Pound Secty. Economics
and Kra belongs to Kra, and Pukti to Pukti
crossfertilization of Blok and Artaud
Van Gogh's Ear on the currency
no more propaganda for monsters
and poets should stay out of politics or become monsters
I have become monsterous with politics
the Russian poet undoubtedly monsterous in his secret
      notebook
Tibet should be left alone
These are obvious prophecies
America will be destroyed
Russian poets will struggle with Russia
Whitman warned against this "fabled Damned of nations"
Where was Theodore Roosevelt when he sent out ultimatums
      from his castle in Camden
Where was the House of Representatives when Crane read
      aloud from his prophetic books
What was Wall Street scheming when Lindsay announced
      the doom of Money

Were they listening to my ravings in the locker rooms of
    Bickfords Employment Offices?
Did they bend their ears to the moans of my soul when I
    struggled with market research statistics in the Forum
    at Rome?
No they were fighting in fiery offices, on carpets of heartfail-
    ure, screaming and bargaining with Destiny
fighting the Skeleton with sabers, muskets, buck teeth,
    indigestion, bombs of larceny, whoredom, rockets,
    pederasty,
back to the wall to build up their wives and apartments, lawns,
    suburbs, fairydoms,
Puerto Ricans crowded for massacre on 114th St. for the sake
    of an imitation Chinese-Moderne refrigerator
Elephants of mercy murdered for the sake of an Elizabethan
    birdcage
millions of agitated fanatics in the bughouse for the sake of
    the screaming soprano of industry
Money-chant of soapers—toothpaste apes in television sets—
    deodorizers on hypnotic chairs—
petroleum mongers in Texas—jet plane streaks among the clouds—
sky writers liars in the face of Divinity—fanged butchers of
    hats and shoes, all Owners! Owners! Owners! with
    obsession on property and vanishing Selfhood!
and their long editorials on the fence of the screaming negro
    attacked by ants crawled out of the front page!
Machinery of a mass electrical dream! A war-creating Whore
    of Babylon bellowing over Capitols and Academies!

Money! Money! Money! shrieking mad celestial money of
    illusion! Money made of nothing, starvation, suicide!
    Money of failure! Money of death!
Money against Eternity! and eternity's strong mills grind out
    vast paper of Illusion!

Paris, December 1957

Television Was a Baby Crawling Toward That Deathchamber

It is here, the long Awaited bleap-blast light that Speaks one
    red tongue like Politician, but happy its own govt.,
either we blow ourselves up now and die, like the old tribe of
    man, arguing among neutrons, spit on India, fuck Tibet,
    stick up America, clobber Moscow, die Baltic, have your
    tuberculosis in Arabia, wink not in Enkidu's reverie—
it's a long Train of Associations stopped for gas in the desert
    & looking for drink of old-time H_2O—
made up of molecules, it ends being innocent as Lafcadio
    afraid to get up & cook his bacon—
I prophesy: the Pigs won't mind! I prophesy: Death will be old
    folks home!
I prophesy: Chango will prophesy on national Broadcasting
    System,
I prophesy, we will all prophesy to each other & I give thee
    happy tidings Robert Lowell and Jeanette MacDonald—
Dusty moonlight, Starbeam riding its own flute, soul revealed
    in the scribble, an ounce of looks, an Invisible Seeing,
    Hope, The Vanisher betokening Eternity
one finger raised warning above his gold eyeglasses—and Mozart
    playing giddy-note an hour on the Marxist gramophone—
All Be—let the Kabbalah star be formed of perfect circles in a
    room of 1950 unhappiness where Myrna Loy gets lost—

The Bardo Thodol extends in the millions of black jello for
        every dying Mechanic—We will make Colossal movies—
We will be a great Tantric Mogul & starify a new Hollywood
        with our unimaginable Flop—Great Paranoia!
The Family presents, your Corpse Hour—attended by myriad
        flies—hyperactive Commentators freed at their most
        bestial—sneering literary—perhaps a captive & loan Square
caught hiding behind a dummy-univac in the obscurest Morgues
        of Hearst—wherever—no more possible—
Only remains, a photo of a riverswollen hand in black and white,
        arm covered by aged burlap to the wrist—
skin peeling from the empty fingers—; yet discovered by a mad
        Negro high on tea & solitary enough himself to notice a Fate—
therefore, with camera remembered and passed along by hand
        mail roaring Jet toward Chicago, Big Table empty this
        morning,
nothing but an old frog-looking editor worried about his
        Aesthetics,
That's life Kulchur '61—retired to New York to invent Morse
        Code & found a great yellow Telegraph—
Merry Xmas Paul carroll and irving Rose in Thrall—give up
        thy song & flower to any passing Millennium!
I am the One, you are the One, we are the One, A. Hitler's
        One as well as fast as his Many heavenly Jews are reborn,
many a being with a nose—and many with none but an ear
        somewhere next to a Yelling Star—
I myself saw the sunflower-monkeys of the Moon—spending
        their dear play-money electricity in a homemade tape-
        record minute of cartoony high Sound—

goodbye Farewell repeated by Wagner Immortal in many a
	gladdened expanding mid-europe Hour
that I'll be hearing forever if the world I go to's Music, Yes good
	to be stuck thru Eternity on that aching Liebestod Note
which has been playing out there always for me, whoever can
	hear enough to write it down for a day to let men fiddle in
	space, blow a temporary brass tuba or wave a stick at a
	physical orchestra
and remember the Wagner-music in his own titty-head
	Consciousness—ah yes that's the message—
That's what I came here to compose, what I knocked off my life
	to Inscribe on my gray metal typewriter,
borrowed from somebody's lover's mother got it from Welfare,
	all interconnected and gracious a bunch of Murderers
as possible in this Kalpa of Hungry blood-drunkard Ghosts—
	We all have to eat—us Beings
gnaw bones, suck marrow, drink living white milk from
	heavenly Breasts or from bucktoothed negress or
	wolf-cow.
The sperm bodies wriggle in pools of vagina, in Yin, that reality
	we must have spasmed our Beings upon—
The brothers and sisters die if we live, the Myriads Invisible
	squeak reptile complaint
on Memory's tail which us pterodactyl-buzzard-dove-descended
	two foot mammal-born Geek-souls almost Forget—
Grab—a cock—any eye—bright hair—All Memory & All
	Eternity now, reborn as One—
no loss to those—the Peacock spreads its cosmic-eye Magnificat-
	feathered tail over its forgotten Ass—

The being roars its own name in the Radio, the Bomb goes off its
    twenty years ago,
I hear thy music O my mystery, my Father in myself, my mother in
    my eye, brother in my hand, sister-in-honey on my own
    Poetry's Tongue, my Hallelujah Way beyond all mortal
    inherited Heavens, O my own blind ancient Love-in-mind!
Who? but us all, a Me, a One, a Dying Being, The presence, now,
    this desk, hand running over the steps of imagination
over the letter-ladders on machine, vibrating humm-herald
    Extend-hope own unto Thee, returning infinite-myriad at the
    Heart, that is only red blood,
that is where murder is still innocence, that life ate, the white
    plasmic monsters forage in their fleet Macrocosm—bit apple
    or black huge bacteria gods loomed out of nowhere, potent
maybe once victorious on Saturn in dinosaur-inspired messy
    old hallucinated war—
same battle raging in tsraved cats and gahgard dogs for American
    ghostly bone—man and man, fairy against red, black on white
    on white, with teeth going to the dentist to escape in gas—
The President laughs in his Chair, and swivels his head on his neck
    controlling fangs of Number—
bacteria come numberless, atoms count themselves greatness in
    their pointy Empire—
Russian Neutrons spy on all Conspiracy—& Chinese yellow
    energy waves have ocean and Empyrean ready against
    attack & future starvation—Korean principalities of Photon
    are doubles in all but name—differing Wizards of Art of
    Electron divide as many as tribes of Congo—Africa's a
    vast jail of Shadows—I am not I,

my molecules are numbered, mirrored in all Me Robot Seraphy
     parts, cock-creator navel-marked, Eye Seer with delicate
     breasts, teeth & gullet to ingest the living dove-life
foreimage of the Self-Maw Death Is Now;—but there is the
     Saintly Meat of the Heart—feeling to thee o Peter and all
     my Lords—Decades American loves car-rides and
     vow-sworn faces lain on my breast,—my head on many
     more naked than my own sad hoping flesh—
our feelings! come back to the heart—to the old blind hoping
     Creator home in Mercy, beating everywhere behind
     machine hand clothes-man Senator iron powerd or
     fishqueen fugitive-com'd lapel—

Here I am—Old Betty Boop whoopsing behind the skull-
     microphone wondering what Idiot soap opera horror show
     we broadcast by Mistake—full of communists and franken-
     stein cops and
mature capitalists running the State Department and the Daily
     News Editorial hypnotizing millions of legional-eyed
     detectives to commit mass murder on the Invisible
which is only a bunch of women weeping hidden behind news-
     papers in the Andes, conspired against by Standard Oil,
which is a big fat fairy monopolizing all Being that has form'd
     it self to Oil,
and nothing gets in its way so it grabs different oils in all poor
     mystic aboriginal Principalities too weak to
Screech out over the radio that Standard Oil is a bunch of
     spying Businessmen intent on building one Standard Oil in
     the whole universe like an egotistical cancer

and yell on Television to England to watch out for United
    Fruits they got Central America by the balls
nobody but them can talk San Salvador, they run big Guate-
    mala puppet armies, gas Dictators, they're the Crown
    of Thorns
upon the Consciousness of poor Christ-indian Central America,
    and the Pharisees are US Congress & Publicans is the
    American People
who have driven righteous bearded faithful pink new Castro
    1961 is he mad? who knows—Hope for him, he stay true
& his wormy 45-year dying peasants teach Death's beauty sugar
    beyond politics, build iron children schools
for alphabet molecule stars, that mystic history & giggling
    revolution henceforth no toothless martyrs be memorized
    by some pubescent Juan who'll smoke my marijuana—
Turn the Teacher on!—Yes not conspire dollars under navy-
    town board marijuana walk, not spy vast Services
    of gunny Secrecy under drear eyeglass Dulles to
    ASSASSINATE!
INVADE! STARVE OUT! SUPPLY INVISIBLE ARMS!
    GIVE MONEY TO ORGANIZE DEATH FOR
    CUBAN REVOLUTION! BLOCKADE WHAT
    FRAIL MACHINERY!
MAKE EVIL PROPAGANDA OVER THE WORLD!
    ISOLATE THE FAITHFUL'S SOUL! TAKE ALL
    RICHES BACK! BE WORLDLY PRINCE AND
    POWER OVER THE UNBELIEVABLE! MY GOD!
AMERICA WILL BE REFUSED ETERNITY BY HER
    OWN MAD SON THE BOMB! MEN WORKING IN

ELECTRICITY BE US SADISTS THEIR MAGIC
PHANOPOEIAC THRU MASS MEDIA THE
NASTIEST IN THIS FIRST HISTORY!
EVIL SPELLS THRU THE DAILY NEWS! HORRIBLE
MASOCHISMS THUNK UP BY THE AMERICAN
MEDICAL ASSOCIATION! DEATH TO JUNKIES
THRU THE TREASURY DEPARTMENT! TAXES
ON YOUR HATE FOR THIS HERE WAR!
LEGIONS OF DECENCY BLACKMAIL THY CIN-
EMAL FATE! CONSPIRACIES CONTROL ALL
WHITE MAGICIANS! I CAN'T TELL YOU MY
SECRET STORY ON TV!
Chambers of Commerce misquote Bob Hope who is a grim
sex revolutionist talking in hysterical code flat awful jokes
Jimmy Durante's kept from screaming to death in the movies
by a huge fat Cardinal, the Spell Man, Black Magician he
won't let mad white Chaplin talk thru the State Mega-
phone! He takes evil pix with Swiss financial cunt!
It's the American Medical Association poisoning the poets with
their double-syndicate of heroin cut with money-dust,
Military psychiatrists make deathly uniforms it's Tanganyikan
nerve-skin in the submarinic navy they're prepared for
eternal solitude, once they go down they turn to Reptiles
Human dragons trained to fly the air with bomb-claws
clutched to breast & wires entering their brains thru
muffled ears—connected to what control tower—jacked
to what secret Lab where the macrocosm-machine
picks up vibrations of my thought in this poem—the attendant
is afraid—Is the President listening? is

Evil Eye, the invisible police-cop-secrecy masters Controlling
　　　　Central Intelligence—do they know I took Methedrine,
　　　　heroin, magic mushrooms, & lambchops & guess
　　　　toward a Prophecy tonight?
No the big dopes all they do is control each other—Doom!
　　　　in the vast car America—they're screeching on two
　　　　mind-wheels on a National Curve—the Car that's
　　　　made to die by Mr. Inhuman
Moneyhand, by advertising nastyhead Inc. Dream Cancer Prexy
　　　　Owner Distributor Publisher & TV Doctor of Emotional
　　　　Breakdown—he told that Mayor to get in that car without
　　　　his pubic hair and drive to Kill get to Las Vegas so the
　　　　oldfashioned jewish communists
wouldn't get their idealistic radio program on the air in time
　　　　to make everybody cry in the desert for the Indian
　　　　Serpent to come
back from the Oklahoma mound where he hid with his
　　　　15,000,000 visionary original Redskin patriot-wives and
　　　　warriors—they made up one big mystic serpent with
　　　　its tail-a-mouth like a lost Tibet
MURDERED AND DRIVEN FROM THE EARTH BY US
　　　　JEWISH GOYIM who spend fifty billion things a year—
　　　　things things!—to make the things-machinery that's turned
　　　　the worlds of human consciousness into a thing of War
wherever and whoever is plugged in by real filaments or
　　　　wireless or whatever magic wordy-synapse to the money-
　　　　center of the mind
whose Eye is hidden somewhere behind All mass media—
　　　　what makes reporters fear their secret dreamy

news—behind the Presidential mike & all its starry bunting,
    front for some mad BILLIONAIRES
who own United Fruits & Standard Oil and Hearst The Press
    and Texas NBC and someone owns the Radios owns vast
    Spheres of Air—Subliminal Billionaire got
State Legislatures filled with Capital Punishment Fiends because
    nobody's been in love on US soil long enough to realize We
    who pay the Public Hangman make State Murder thru
    Alien Gas who cause any form of hate-doom hanging
do that in public everybody agreed by the neck suffering utmost
    pangs Each citizen himself unloved suicides him, because
    there's no beloved, now in America for All in the gas
    chamber the whole California Legislature
screaming because it's Death here—we're so hopeless—The
    Soul of America died with ugly Chessman—strange saintly
    average madman driven to think for his own killers, in his
    pants and shirt with human haircut, said NO to—like a
    Cosmic NO—from the One Mouth of America speaking
    life or death—looked in the eye by America—
Ah what a cold monster OneEye he must've saw thru the
    Star-Spangled Banner & Hollywood with ugly smile
    forbidden movie & old heartless Ike in the White House
    officially allowing Chatterley attacked by Fed Lawyers—
vast Customs agencies searching books—who Advises what
    book where—who invented what's dirty? The Pope?
    Baruch?—tender Genet burned by middleaged vice Officers
sent out by The Automatic Sourface mongers whatever bad
    news he can high up from imaginary Empires name
    Scripps-Howard—just more drear opinions—Damn that

World Telegram was Glad Henry Miller's depression Cancer-
        book not read to sad eyeglass Joe messenger to Grocer
in Manhattan, or candystore emperor Hersh Silverman in
        Bayonne, dreaming of telling the *Truth*, but his Karma
        is selling jellybeans & being kind,
The Customs police denyd him his Burroughs they defecated
        on de Sade, they jack'd off, and tortured his copy of
        Sodom with Nitric Acid in a backroom furnace house at
        Treasury Bureau, pouring Fire on the soul of Rochester,
Warlocks, Black magicians burning and cursing the Love-
        Books, Jack be damned, casting spells from the shores of
        America on the inland cities, lacklove-curses on our Eyes
        which read genital poetry—
O deserts of deprivation for some high school'd gang, lone
        Cleveland that delayed its books of Awe, Chicago strug-
        gling to read its magazines, police and papers yapping
        over grimy gossip skyscraped from some sulphurous
        yellow cloud drift in from archtank hot factories make
        nebulous explosives near Detroit—smudge got on
        Corso's Rosy Page—
US Postmaster, first class sexfiend his disguise told everyone to
        open letters stop the photographic fucks & verbal
        suckeries & lickings of the asshole by tongues meant but
        for poison glue on envelopes Report this privileged
        communication to Yours Truly We The National Police—
        We serve you once a day—you humanical meat creephood—
and yearly the national furnace burned much book, 2,000,000
        pieces mail, one decade unread propaganda from Vietnam
        & Chinese mag harangues, Engelian

dialectics handmade in Gobi for proud export to top hat & tails Old
Bones in his penthouse on a skyscraper in Manhattan, laconic
on two phones that rang thru the nets of money over earth,
as he barked his orders to Formosa for more spies, abhorred
all Cuba sugar from concourse with Stately stomachs—
That's when I began vomiting my paranoia when Old National
Skullface the invisible sixheaded billionaire began brainwash-
ing my stomach with strange feelers in the *Journal
American*—the penis of billionaires depositing professional
semen in my ear, Fulton Lewis *coming* with strychnine jizzum
in his voice making an evil suggestion that entered my mouth
while I was sitting there gaping in wild dubiety & astound on my
peaceful couch, he said to all the taxidrivers and schoolteach-
ers in brokendown old Blakean America
that Julius and Ethel Rosenberg smelled bad & shd die, he sent to
kill them with personal electricity, his power station is the
spirit of generation leaving him thru his asshole by Error, that
very electric entered Ethel's eye
and his tongue is the prick of a devil he don't even know, a
magic capitalist ghosting it on the lam after the Everett
Massacre—fucks a Newscaster in the mouth every time
he gets on the Microphone—
and those ghost jizzums started my stomach trouble with capital
punishment, Ike chose to make an Artificial Death for them
poor spies—if they were spying on me? who cares?—Ike
disturbed the balance of the cosmos by his stroke-head
deathshake, 'NO'
It was a big electrocution in every paper and mass medium,
Television was a baby crawling toward that deathchamber

Later quiz shows prepared the way for egghead omelet, I was
    rotten, I was the egghead that spoiled the last supper,
    they made me vomit more—whole programs of
    halfeaten comedians sliming out my Newark Labor
    Leaders' assholes
They used to wash them in the '30s with Young Politics Ideas,
    I was too young to smell anything but my own secret
    mind, I didn't even know assholes basic to Modern
    Democracy—What can we teach our negroes now?
That they are Negroes, that I am thy Jew & thou my white
    Goy & him Chinese?—They think they're Arab
    Macrocosms now!
My uncle thinks his Truthcloud's Jewish—thinks his Name is
    Nose-smell-Newark 5 decades—& that's all except there's
    Gentile Images of mirrory vast Universe—
and Chinese Microcosms too, a race of spade microcosms apart,
    like Jewish truth clouds & Goyishe Nameless Vasts
But I am the Intolerant One Gasbag from the Morgue & Void,
    Garbler of all Conceptions that myope my eye & is Uncle
    Sam asleep in the Funeral Home—?
Bad magic, scram, hide in J. E. Hoover's bathingsuit. Make his
    pants fall in the ocean, near Miami—
Gangster CRASH! America will be forgotten, the identity files
    of the FBI slipt into the void-crack, the fingerprints
    unwhorled—no track where He came from—
Man left no address, not even hair, just disappeared & Forgot his
    big wallstreet on Earth—Uncle I hate the FBI it's all a big
    dreamy skyscraper somewhere over the Mutual Network—
    I don't even know who they are—like the Nameless—

Hallooo I am coming end of my Presidency—Everybody's
    fired—I am a hopeless whitehaired congressman—I lost my
    last election—landslide for Reader's Digest—not even humans—
Nobody home in town—just offices with many jangling
        telephones & automatic switchboards keep the message—
        typewriters return yr calls oft, Yakkata yak &
        tinbellring—THE POLICE ARE AT THE DOOR—
What are you doing eccentric in this solitary office? a mad
        vagrant Creep Truthcloud sans identity card—It's
        Paterson allright—anyway the people disappeared—
        downtown Fabian Bldg. branch office for The Chamber
        of Commerce runs the streetlights
all thru dark winter rain by univac piped from Washington
        Lobby—they've abolished the streets from the universe—
        just keep control of
the lights—in case of ectoplasm trafficking thru dead Market—
        where the Chinese restaurant usta play Muzak in the early
        century—soft green rugs & pastel walls—perfumèd tea—
Goodbye, said the metal Announcer in doors of The Chamber
        of Commerce—we're merging with NAM forever—and
        the NAM has no door but's sealed copper 10 foot vault
        under the Federal Reserve Bldg—
Six billionaires that control America are playing Scrabble with
        antique Tarot—they've just unearthed another Pyramid—
        in the bombproof Cellar at Fort Knox
Not even the FBI knows who—They give orders to J. E.
        Hoover thru the metal phonegirl at the Robot Transmit-
        ter on top of RCA—you

can see new Fortune officers look like spies from 20 floors
    below with their eyeglasses & gold skulls—silver teeth
    flashing up the shit-mouthed grin—weeping in their
    martinis! There is no secret to the success of the
Six Billionaires that own all Time since the Gnostic Revolt in
    Aegypto—they built the Sphinx to confuse my sex life,
    Who Fuckd the Void?
Why are they starting that war all over again in Laos over
    Neutral Mind? Is the United States CIA army Legions
    overthrowing somebody like Angelica Balabanoff?
Six thousand movietheaters, 100,000,000 television sets, a
    billion radios, wires and wireless crisscrossing hemi-
    spheres, semaphore lights and Morse, all telephones
    ringing at once connect every mind by its ears to one
    vast consciousness This Time Apocalypse—everybody
    waiting for one mind to break thru—
Man-prophet with two eyes Dare all creation with his
    dying tongue & say I AM—Messiah swallow back his
    death into his stomach, gaze thru great pupils of his
    Bodies' eyes
and look in each Eye man, the eyeglassed fearful byriad-look
    that might be Godeyes see thru Death—that now are
    clark & ego reading manlaw—write newsbroadcasts
    to cover with Fears their
own Messiah that must come when all of us conscious—
    Breakthru to all other Consciousness to say the Word I
    Am as spoken by a certain God—Millennia knew and
    waited till this one Century –

29

Now all sentience broods and listens—contemplative & hair
   full of rain for 15 years inside New York—what millions
   know and hark to hear, & death will tell, but—
many strange magicians in buildings listening inside their own
   heads—or clouds over Manhattan Bridge—or strained
   thru music messages to—I Am from the central One!
   Come
blow the Cosmic Horn to waken every Tiglon & Clown
   sentience throughout the vasting circus—in the Name of
   God pick up the telephone call Networks announcing
   Suchness That—
I Am mutter a million old Gods in their beards, that had been
   sleeping at evening radios—cackling in their Larynx—
   Talking to myself again
said the Messiah turning a dial to remember his last
   broadcast—I scare myself, I eat my hand, I swallow my
   own head, I stink in the inevitable bathroom of death this
   Being requires—O Widen the Area of Consciousness! O
set my Throne in Space, I rise to sit in the midst of the Starry
   Visible!—Calling All Beings! in dirt from the ant to the
   most frightened Prophet that ever clomb tower to vision
   planets
crowded in one vast space ship toward Andromeda—That all
   lone soul in Iowa or Hark-land join the Lone, set forth,
   walk naked like a Hebrew king, enter the human cities
   and speak free,
at last the Man-God come that hears all Phantasy behind the
   matter-babble in his ear, and walks out of his Cosmic
   Dream into the cosmic street

open mouth to the First Consciousness—God's woke up now,
   you Seraphim, call men with trumpet microphone &
   telegraph, hail every sleepwalker with Holy Name,

Life is waving, the cosmos is sending a message to itself, its
   image is reproduced endlessly over TV
over the radio the babble of Hitler's and Claudette Colbert's
   voices got mixed up in the bathroom radiator
Hello hello are you the Telephone the Operator's singing we
   are the daughters of the universe
get everybody on the line at once plug in all being ears by
   loudspeaker, newspeak, secret messàge,
handwritten electronic impulse traveling along rays electric
   spiderweb
magnetisms shuddering on one note We We We, mustached
   disc jockeys trembling in mantric excitement, flowery
   patterns bursting over the broken couch,
drapes falling to the floor in St. John Perse's penthouse,
   Portugal's water is running in all the faucets on the SS
   Santa Maria,
chopping machines descend on the pre-dawn tabloid, the wire
   services are hysterical and send too much message,
they're waiting to bam out the Armageddon, millions of rats
   reported in China, smoke billows out New York's hospital
   furnace smokestack,
I am writing millions of letters a year, I correspond with
   hopeful messengers in Detroit, I am taking drugs
and leap at my postman for more correspondence, Man is
   leaving the earth in a rocket ship,

there is a mutation of the race, we are no longer human beings,
	we are one being, we are being connected to itself,
it makes me crosseyed to think how, the mass media assemble
	themselves like congolese Ants for a purpose
in the massive clay mound an undiscovered huge Queen is
	born, Africa wakes to redeem the old Cosmos,
I am masturbating in my bed, I dreamed a new Stranger
	touched my heart with his eye,
he hides in a sidestreet loft in Hoboken, the heavens have
	covered East Second Street with Snow,
all day I walk in the wilderness over white carpets of City, we
	are redeeming ourself, I am born,
the Messiah woke in the Universe, I announce the New Nation,
	in every mind, take power over the dead creation,
I am naked in New York, a star breaks thru the blue skull of the
	sky out the window,
I seize the tablets of the Law, the spectral Buddha and the spec-
	tral Christ turn to a stick of shit in the void, a fearful Idea,
I take the crown of the Idea and place it on my head, and sit a
	King beside the reptile Devas of my Karma—
Eye in every forehead sleeping waxy & the light gone inward—
	to dream of fearful Jaweh or the Atom Bomb—
All these eternal spirits to be wakened, all these bodies touched
	and healed, all these lacklove
suffering the Hate, dumbed under rainbows of Creation, O
	Man the means of Heaven are at hand, thy rocks & my
	rocks are nothing,
the identity of the Moon is the identity of the flower-thief, I
	and the Police are one in revolutionary Numbness!

Yawk, Mercy The Octopus, it's IT cometh over the Void &
      makes whistle its lonemouthed Flute You-me forever—
Stop Arguing, Cosmos, I give up so I be, I receive a happy
      letter from Ray Bremser exiled from home in New Jersey
      jail—

Clocks are abuilding for a thousand years, ticking behind
      metalloidesque electronico-clankered industries smokeless
      in silent mind city—
Dawn of the Ages! Man thy Alarm rings thru sweet myriad
      mornings in every desperate-carred street! Saints wait in
      each metropolis
for Message to Assassinate the old idea, that 20,000 yr old
      eye-god Man thought was Being Secret mystery,
unbearable Judge above, God alien handless tongueless to
      poor man, who'll scream for mercy on his deathbed—Oh
      I saw that black
Octopus Death, with supernatural antennae spikes raying
      Awful waves at my consciousness, huge blind Ball
      invisible behind the rooms in the universe—a not-a-
      man—a no-one—
      Nobodaddy—
Omnipotent Telepath more visionary than my own Prophetics
      & Memories—Reptile-sentient shimmer-feel-hole Here,
Dense Soullessness wiser than Time, the Eater-Darkness
      hungry for All—but must wait till I leave my body to
      enter that
One Mind nebula to my recollection—Implacable, my soul
      dared not die,

Shrank back from the leprous door-mind in its breast, touch
    Him and the hand's destroyed,
Death God in the End, before the Timeworld of creation—I
    mean some kind of monster from another dimension is
    eating Beings of our own Cosmos—
I saw him try to make me leave my corpse-illusion Allen, myth
    movie world come to celluloid-end,
I screamed seeing myself in reels of death my consciousness a
    cinematic toy played once in faded attick by man-already-
    forgotten
His orphan starhood inked from Space, the movie industry
    itself blot up its History & all wracked myriad Epics,
    Space wiped itself out,
lost in a wall-crack dream itself had once disappearing—
    maybe trailing endless comet-long trackless thru what
    unwonted dimensions it keeps dreaming existence can
    die inside of—vanish this Cosmos of Stars I am turning
    to bones in—
That much illusion, and what's visions but visions, and these
    words filled Methedrine—I have a backache & 2 tel-
    egrams come midnight from messengers that cry to plug
    in the Electrode Ear to
my skull downstreet, & hear what they got to say, big lives like
    trees of Cancer in Bronx & Long Island—Telephones
    connect the voids island blissy darkness scattered in many
    manmind—

New York, February 1961

I Am a Victim of Telephone

When I lie down to sleep dream the Wishing Well it rings
"Have you a new play for the brokendown theater?"
When I write in my notebook poem it rings
"Buster Keaton is under the brooklyn bridge on Frankfurt
    and Pearl . . ."
When I unsheath my skin extend my cock toward someone's
    thighs fat or thin, boy or girl
Tingaling—"Please get him out of jail . . . the police are
    crashing down"
When I lift the soupspoon to my lips, the phone on the floor
    begins purring
"Hello it's me—I'm in the park two broads from Iowa . . .
    nowhere to sleep last night . . . hit 'em in the mouth"
When I muse at smoke crawling over the roof outside my
    street window
purifying Eternity with my eye observation of gray vaporous
    columns in the sky
ring ring "Hello this is Esquire be a dear and finish your
    political commitment manifesto"
When I listen to radio presidents roaring on the convention
    floor
the phone also chimes in "Rush up to Harlem with us and
    see the riots"

Always the telephone linked to all the hearts of the world
        beating at once
crying my husband's gone my boyfriend's busted forever my
        poetry was rejected
won't you come over for money and please won't you write
        me a piece of bullshit
How are you dear can you come to Easthampton we're all
        here bathing in the ocean we're all so lonely
and I lie back on my pallet contemplating $50 phone bill,
        broke, drowsy, anxious, my heart fearful of the fingers
        dialing, the deaths, the singing of telephone bells
ringing at dawn ringing all afternoon ringing up midnight
        ringing now forever.

New York, June 20, 1964

Mind Breaths

Thus crosslegged on round pillow sat in Teton Space—
I breathed upon the aluminum microphone-stand a body's
    length away
I breathed upon the teacher's throne, the wooden chair with
    yellow pillow
I breathed further, past the sake cup half emptied by the
    breathing guru
Breathed upon the green sprigged thick-leaved plant in a
    flowerpot
Breathed upon the vast plateglass shining back th' assembled
    sitting Sangha in the meditation cafeteria
my breath thru nostril floated out to the moth of evening
    beating into window'd illumination
breathed outward over aspen twigs trembling September's top
    yellow leaves twilit at mountain foot
breathed over the mountain, over snowpowdered crags ringed
    under slow-breathed cloud-mass white spumes
windy across Tetons to Idaho, gray ranges under blue space
    swept
with delicate snow flurries, breaths Westward
mountain grass trembling in tiny winds toward Wasatch
Breezes south late autumn in Salt Lake's wooden temple streets,
white salt dust lifted swirling by the thick leaden lake, dust
    carried up over Kennecott's pit onto the massive Unit Rig,

37

out towards Reno's neon, dollar bills skittering downstreet
    along the curb,
up into Sierras oak leaves blown down by fall cold chills
over peaktops snowy gales beginning,
a breath of prayer down on Kitkitdizze's horngreen leaves
    close to ground,
over Gary's tile roof, over temple pillar, tents and manzanita
    arbors in Sierra pine foothills—
a breath falls over Sacramento Valley, roar of wind down the
    sixlane freeway across Bay Bridge
uproar of papers floating over Montgomery Street, pigeons
    flutter down before sunset from Washington Park's white
    churchsteeple—
Golden Gate waters whitecapped scudding out to Pacific
    spreads
over Hawaii a balmy wind thru Hotel palmtrees, a moist
    warmth swept over the airbase, a dank breeze in Guam's
    rotten Customs shed,
clear winds breathe on Fiji's palm & coral shores, by
    wooden hotels in Suva town flags flutter, taxis whoosh
    by Friday night's black promenaders under the rock &
    roll discotheque window upstairs beating with English
    neon—
on a breeze into Sydney, and across hillside grass where
    mushrooms lie low on Cow-Flops in Queensland, down
    Adelaide's alleys a flutter of music from Brian Moore's
    Dobro carried in the wind—
up thru Darwin Land, out Gove Peninsula green ocean breeze,
    clack of Yerkalla village song sticks by the trembling wave

Yea and a wind over mercurial waters of Japan North East, a
        hollow wooden gong echoes in Kyoto's temple hall
        below the graveyard's wavy grass
A foghorn blowing in the China Sea, torrential rains over
        Saigon, bombers float over Cambodia, visioned tiny from
        stone Avelokitesvera's many-faced towers Angkor Wat in
        windy night,
a puff of opium out of a mouth yellowed in Bangkok, a puff
        of hashish flowing thick out of a bearded saddhu's
        nostrils & eyes in Nimtallah Burning Ghat,
wood smoke flowing in wind across Hooghly Bridge, incense
        wafted under the Bo Tree in Bodh Gaya, in Benares
        woodpiles burn at Manikarnika returning incensed
        souls to Shiva,
wind dallies in the amorous leaves of Brindaban, still air on the
        vast mosque floor above Old Delhi's alleyways,
wind blowing over Kausani town's stone wall, Himalayan
        peaktops ranged hundreds of miles along snowy horizon,
        prayer flags flutter over Almora's wood brown
        housetops,
trade winds carry dhows thru Indian Ocean to Mombasa or
        down to Dar 'Salaam's riverside sail port, palms sway &
        sailors wrapped in cotton sleep on log decks—
Soft breezes up thru Red Sea to Eliat's dry hotels, paper
        leaflets scatter by the Wailing Wall, drifting into the
        Sepulchre
Mediterranean zephyrs leaving Tel Aviv, over Crete, Lassithi
        Plains' windmills still turn the centuries near Zeus'
        birth cave

Piraeus wave-lashed, Venice lagoon's waters blown up over the
    floor of San Marco, Piazza flooded and mud on the
    marble porch, gondolas bobbing up & down choppy
    waters at the Zattere,
chill September fluttering thru Milan's Arcade, cold bones &
    overcoats flapping in St. Peter's Square,
down Appian Way silence by gravesites, stelae stolid on a
    lonely grass path, the breath of an old man laboring up road—
Across Scylla & Charybdis, Sicilian tobacco smoke wafted
    across the boat deck,
into Marseilles coalstacks black fumes float into clouds,
    steamer's white drift spume down wind all the way to
    Tangier,
a breath of red-tinged Autumn in Provence, boats slow on the
    Seine, the lady wraps her cloak tight round her bodice on
    toppa Eiffel Tower's iron head—
across the Channel rough black-green waves, in London's
    Piccadilly beer cans roll on concrete neath Eros' silver
    breast, the Sunday Times lifts and settles on wet fountain
    steps—
over Iona Isle blue day and balmy Inner Hebrides breeze, fog
    drifts across Atlantic,
Labrador white frozen blowing cold, down New York's
    canyons manila paper bags scurry toward Wall from
    Lower East side—
a breath over my Father's head in his apartment on Park
    Avenue Paterson,
a cold September breeze down from East Hill, Cherry Valley's
    maples tremble red,

40

out thru Chicago Windy City the vast breath of Consciousness
      dissolves, smokestacks and autos drift expensive fumes
      ribboned across railroad tracks,
Westward, a single breath blows across the plains, Nebraska's
      fields harvested & stubble bending delicate in evening airs
up Rockies, from Denver's Cherry Creekbed another zephyr
      risen,
across Pike's Peak an icy blast at sunset, Wind River peaktops
      flowing toward the Tetons,
a breath returns vast gliding grass flats cow-dotted into
      Jackson Hole, into a corner of the plains,
up the asphalt road and mud parking lot, a breeze of restless
      September, up wood stairways in the wind
into the cafeteria at Teton Village under the red tram lift
a calm breath, a silent breath, a slow breath breathes outward
      from the nostrils.

September 28, 1973

Fourth Floor, Dawn,
Up All Night Writing Letters

Pigeons shake their wings on the copper church roof
out my window across the street, a bird perched on the cross
surveys the city's blue-gray clouds. Larry Rivers
'll come at 10 A.M. and take my picture. I'm taking
your picture, pigeons. I'm writing you down, Dawn.
I'm immortalizing your exhaust, Avenue A bus.
O Thought, now you'll have to think the same thing forever!

New York, June 7, 1980, 6:48 A.M.

Love Comes

I lay down to rest
weary at best
of party life
& dancing nights
Alone, Prepared
all I dared
bed & oil
bath, small toil
to clean my feet
place my slippers neat.

Alone, despair—lighthearted, bare-
bottom trudged about,
listening the shout
of students down below
rock rolling fast and slow
shaking ash for show,
or love, or joy
hairless girl and boy
goldenhaired goy.

The door creaked loud
far from the crowd
Upstairs he trod

Eros or some god
come to visit,
Washed in the bath
calm as death
patient took a shit
approached me clean
naked serene

I sat on his thighs
looked in his eyes
I touched his hair
Bare body there
head to foot
big man root
I kissed his chest
Came down from above
I took in his rod
he pushed and shoved
That felt best

My behind in his groin
his big boyish loin
stuck all the way in
That's how we began
Both knees on the bed
his head to my head
he shoved in again
I loved him then

I pushed back deep
Soon he wanted to sleep
He wanted to rest
my back to his chest
My rear went down
I rolled it around
He pushed to the bottom
Now I've got 'em
He took control
made the bed roll

I relaxed my inside
loosed the ring in my hide
Surrendered in time
whole body and mind
and heart at the sheet
He continued to beat
his meat in my meat,
held me around
my chest love-bound
sighed without sound

My breast relaxed
my belly a sack
my sphincter loosed
to his hard deep thrust
I clenched my gut tight
in full moon light
thru curtained window

for an hour or so
thin clouds in the sky
I watched pass by
sigh after sigh

He fucked me in the East
he fucked me in the West
he fucked me South
my cock in his mouth
he fucked me North
No sperm shot forth

He continued to love
I spread my knees
pushed apart by his
so that he could move
in and out at ease,
Knelt on the bed
pillow against my head
I wanted release

Tho' it hurt not much
a punishment such
as I asked to feel
back arched for the real
solid prick of control
a youth 19 years old

gave with deep grace,
body fair, curly gold
hair, angelic face

I'd waited a week
the promise he'd keep
if I trusted the truth
of his love in his youth
and I do love him—
tall body, pale skin
Hot heart within
open blue eyes—
a hard cock never lies.

July 4–October 11, 1981

Sphincter

I hope my good old asshole holds out
60 years it's been mostly OK
Tho in Bolivia a fissure operation
     survived the *altiplano* hospital—
a little blood, no polyps, occasionally
     a small hemorrhoid
active, eager, receptive to phallus
     coke bottle, candle, carrot
     banana & fingers—
Now AIDS makes it shy, but still
     eager to serve—
out with the dumps, in with the condom'd
     orgasmic friend—
still rubbery muscular,
     unashamed wide open for joy
But another 20 years who knows,
     old folks got troubles everywhere—
necks, prostates, stomachs, joints—
     I hope the old hole stays young
     till death, relax

March 15, 1986, 1:00 P.M.

48

Personals Ad

"I will send a picture too
if you will send me one of you"

—R. CREELEY

Poet professor in autumn years
seeks helpmate companion protector friend
young lover w/empty compassionate soul
exuberant spirit, straightforward handsome
athletic physique & boundless mind, courageous
warrior who may also like women & girls, no problem,
to share bed meditation apartment Lower East Side,
help inspire mankind conquer world anger & guilt,
empowered by Whitman Blake Rimbaud Ma Rainey &
    Vivaldi,
familiar respecting Art's primordial majesty, priapic carefree
playful harmless slave or master, mortally tender passing
    swift time,
photographer, musician, painter, poet, yuppie or scholar—
Find me here in New York alone with the Alone
going to lady psychiatrist who says Make time in your life
for someone you can call darling, honey, who holds you dear
can get excited & lay his head on your heart in peace.

October 8, 1987

American Sentences 1995–1997

I felt a breeze below my waist and realized that my fly was
open.

April 20, 1995

* * *

Sitting forward elbows on knees, oh what luck! to be able to
crap!

April 17, 1995

'That was good! that was great! That was important!' Standing
to flush the toilet.

June 22, 1995

Relief! relief! O Boy O Boy! That was necessary, wash behind!

January 18, 1997

'A good shit is worth a thousand dollars if your purse can
afford it.'

February 10, 1997, 5 A.M.

Heard at every workplace—obnoxious slogan: "Shit or get
off the pot!"

January 24, 1997

How did I know? How did my ass know? Suddenly, go to the
bathroom!

March 10, 1997

* * *

Château d'Amboise

Sun setting on their faces the diners chatter over plates of
    duck.

                    June 22, 1995

Baul Song

'Oh my mad mind, my mad mind, where've you been all my
    life, my old mad mind?'

                    October 7, 1996

The three-day-old kitchen fly's flown into my bedroom for
    company.

                    December 9, 1996

'Hi-diddly-Dee, a poet's life for me,' Gregory Corso sang in
    Paris sniffing H.

                    January 16, 1997

Chopping apples for the fruit compote—suffer, suffer, suffer,
    suffer!

                    January 24, 1997

Courageous little lemon with so many pits! sliced into the pot.

                    January 25, 1997

The young dog—he jumped out the TV tube stood still then
    barked for supper.

                    January 26, 1997

Stupid of me, stupid of me, just dumb plain stupid ass!
    Where's my pen?

                February 19, 1997, 2:45 A.M.

My father dying of Cancer, head drooping, 'Oy kindelach.'

February 24, 1997

Whatcha do about little girls who want to play Horsey on my
knee?

March 10, 1997

'Hey Buster! Whatcha looking at me like that for?' in the
Bronx subway.

March 10, 1997, 2:45 A.M.

To see Void vast infinite look out the window into the blue sky.

March 23, 1997

C'mon Pigs of Western Civilization Eat More Grease

Eat Eat more marbled Sirloin more Pork'n
      gravy!
Lard up the dressing, fry chicken in
      boiling oil
Carry it dribbling to gray climes, snowed with
      salt,
Little lambs covered with mint roast in racks
      surrounded by roast potatoes wet with
      buttersauce,
Buttered veal medallions in creamy saliva,
      buttered beef, by glistening mountains
      of french fries
Stroganoffs in white hot sour cream, chops
      soaked in olive oil,
surrounded by olives, salty feta cheese, followed
      by Roquefort & Bleu & Stilton
      thirsty
for wine, beer Cocacola Fanta Champagne
      Pepsi retsina arak whiskey vodka
Agh! Watch out heart attack, pop more
      angina pills
order a plate of Bratwurst, fried frankfurters,

couple billion Wimpys', MacDonald's burgers
          to the moon & burp!
Salt on those fries! Hot Dogs! Milkshakes!
Forget greenbeans, everyday a few carrots,
          a mini big spoonful of salty rice'll
          do, make the plate pretty;
throw in some vinegar pickles, briney sauerkraut
          check yr. cholesterol, swallow a pill
and order a sugar Cream donut, pack 2 under
          the size 44 belt
Pass out in the vomitorium come back cough
          up strands of sandwich still chewing
          pastrami at Katz's delicatessen
Back to central Europe & gobble Kielbasa
          in Lódź
swallow salami in Munich with beer, Liverwurst
on pumpernickel in Berlin, greasy cheese in
          a 3 star Hotel near Syntagma, on white
          bread thick-buttered
Set an example for developing nations, salt,
          sugar, animal fat, coffee tobacco Schnapps
Drop dead faster! make room for
          Chinese guestworkers with alien soybean
          curds green cabbage & rice!
Africans Latins with rice beans & calabash can
          stay thin & crowd in apartments for working
          class foodfreaks—

Not like Western cuisine rich in protein
      cancer heart attack hypertension sweat
      bloated liver & spleen megaly
Diabetes & stroke—monuments to carnivorous
      civilizations
presently murdering Belfast
      Bosnia Cypress Ngorno Karabach Georgia
mailing love letter bombs in
      Vienna or setting houses afire
      in East Germany—have another coffee,
      here's a cigar.
And this is a plate of black forest chocolate cake,
      you deserve it.

Athens, December 19, 1993